Honesty: Derek & the Blue Vase

By: Da'Ron Sims

This is a work of fiction. Names, characters, places, and incidents either are the product of the author's imagination or are used fictitiously. Any resemblance to actual persons, living or dead, events, or locales is entirely coincidental.

Published by Veonne Anderson

First paperback edition August 2021

ISBN 978-0-578-96905-3 (paperback)

HONESTY

hon•es•ty

(noun)

According to Webster's dictionary;

1. Honor; honorableness; dignity; propriety; suitableness; decency.

2. The quality or state of being honest; probity; fairness and straightforwardness of conduct, speech, etc.; integrity; sincerity; truthfulness; freedom from fraud or guile.

3. Chastity; modesty.

Derek lives on the south side of Chicago with his mother Rachel and his younger sister Angel.

Derek is seven years old and he is in second grade. Derek is smart and adventurous.

Derek's mother recently celebrated her birthday and one of the gifts she received from one of her friends was a brand blue new vase - which she put on a nightstand in her living room.

Derek's mother told him and his sister not to play with the vase or in the area of the vase...

because it is
very valuable.

One day Derek's mom finds out she has to work late so she asks their neighbors daughter Nicki if she can watch the kids until she gets home.

Derek and his sister decide to play Tag.
Derek tells his sister to run as he counts to 10.

When Derek is finished counting he begins to chase his sister.
Derek chases his sister around the house and eventually into the living room where the blue vase is sitting on the night stand.

Angel sensing her brother is about to catch her, begins to run faster, however, Derek catches up to her and taps her on her back signifying that she is now 'it'...

Unfortunately Derek's tap caused Angel to trip and fall. Angel extended her arms to catch her fall, but she accidently knocks over the vase in the process.

Nicki comes in the living room to check on the kids, and she sees that the vase is broken!

"Are you both alright?"
Nicki asks.
"Yes," they replied.
"Good. Go upstairs and
get ready for bed while I
clean up these
broken pieces."

After Nicki finishes cleaning up the vase, Rachel walks into the door and Nicki explains what happened.

When Nicki leaves, Rachel goes upstairs to her children's rooms to talk to them.
Both of the kids are in their bed wide awake because the fear and guilt of what they did is causing them to lose sleep.

Rachel enters the kid's room and asks,
“what happened to the vase?”

Before Derek can say anything, Angel with tears in her eyes says,

"I knocked the vase over and broke it."

Angel starts crying telling her mother that she didn't mean to do it.

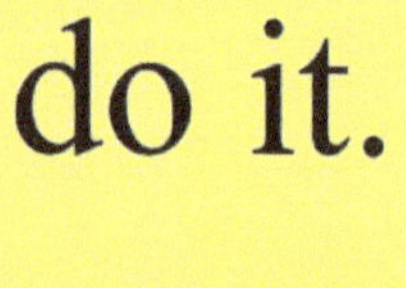

Rachel hugs Angel and tells her it's okay.

Before anything can be said, Derek now with tears in his eyes screams, “it was me!”

Derek looks at his mom and tells her that he and Angel were playing it and when he tapped her on her back, she tripped and knocked the vase over. Derek puts his head down sobbing saying, "It's all my fault." Derek tells his mom to not be mad at Angel because it was an accident.

Rachel looks at Derek and hugs him tightly.

Rachel kiss both Derek and Angel on the forehead and she tells them she loves them both and she is not mad at them.

Both kids look at each other surprised and ask why?
Rachel explains that while she is a little disappointed that the vase is broke; she is happy that her children were honest and told the truth.

Rachel tells her children that no matter what to always be honest about everything and she reads to them 1 John 3:18,

"Dear children, let us not love with words or speech but with actions and in truth."

Derek gives his mom a big hug and tells her that no matter how old he gets he will always be honest and truthful.

About The Author

Da'Ron Radford Sims was born July 28, 1986 in Chicago, IL. Da'Ron grew up on the south side of Chicago and attended several different elementary/grammar schools as a child (including Liberty Temple, Community Christian Academy, Loop Lab & Evangelical Christian School). Da'Ron got saved at the age of 5 and was baptized at the age of 10.

Da'Ron attended Simeon Career Academy high school where he graduated from in 2004. He then attended Robert Morris college where he graduated in 2006 with an associate's degree in Graphic Design & later he attended Roosevelt University where he graduated in 2009 with a bachelor's degree in Communications.

Da'Ron currently works as a Financial Services Coordinator at Heartland Health Centers and he is a member of All Nation Worship Assembly (Chicago location). Da'Ron has a 4 year old daughter whom he loves and hopes to inspire through every thing he does.